DON'T
SQUAT
WITH YOUR
SPURS ON

TEXAS BIX BENDER

DON'T SQUAT

WITH YOUR

SPURS ON

A COWBOY'S

GUIDE TO LIFE

GIBBS SMITH
TO ENRICH AND INSPIRE HUMANKIND
Salt Lake City | Charleston | Santa Fe | Santa Barbara

Revised Edition
25 24 23 22 21   23 22 21 20 19

Published by
Gibbs Smith
P.O. Box 667
Layton, Utah 84041

1.800.835.4993 orders
www.gibbs-smith.com

Design by Black Eye Design
Printed and bound in the U.S.A.
Gibbs Smith books are printed on either recycled, 100 percent post-
consumer waste, FSC-certified papers or on paper produced from a
100 percent certified sustainable forest-controlled wood source.

Library of Congress Cataloging-in-Publication Data

Bender, Texas Bix, 1949-
   Don't squat with your spurs on : a cowboy's guide to life / Texas
Bix Bender. - Rev. ed.
      p. cm.
   Rev. ed. of: Don't squat with yer spurs on! Salt Lake City :
Peregrine Smith Books, 1992.
   ISBN-13: 978-1-4236-0699-4
   ISBN-10: 1-4236-0699-X
 1. Cowboys-West (U.S.)-Humor. 2. West (U.S.)-Social life and
customs-Humor. 3. Cowboys' writings, American-West (U.S.) I.
Bender, Texas Bix, 1949- Don't squat with yer spurs on! II. Title.
  F596.B33 2009
  978-dc22

                          2009017611

ISBN 13: 978-087905-470-0 (first edition)
ISBN 10: 0-87905-470-0 (pb) (first edition)

THE CODE OF THE WEST

Write it in your heart.
Stand by the code, and it will
stand by you. Ask no more and
give no less than honesty, courage,
loyalty, generosity, and fairness.

DON'T NEVER INTERFERE WITH SOMETHING THAT AIN'T BOTHERIN' YOU NONE.

TIMING

has a lot to

do with the

outcome

of a rain

dance.

Every quarrel
is a private one.
Outsiders are
never welcome.

THERE NEVER WAS A HORSE
THAT COULDN'T BE RODE;

THERE NEVER WAS A MAN
THAT COULDN'T BE THROWED.

THERE'S MORE
WAYS TO SKIN
A CAT THAN
STICKIN' HIS
HEAD IN A
BOOT JACK
AND JERKIN'
ON HIS TAIL.

NEVER

ASK A MAN

the size of

his spread.

After weeks
of beans and
taters, even
a change to
taters and
beans is good.

Some ranchers raise pigs and
some will even admit it.

EITHER WAY,
THEY'RE RAISIN' PIGS.

NEVER TAKE TO SAWIN' ON THE BRANCH THAT'S SUPPORTIN' YOU,

UNLESS YOU'RE BEIN' HUNG FROM IT.

NEVER
KICK A
FRESH
TURD
on a hot day.

AFTER EATING AN ENTIRE BULL, a mountain lion felt so good he started roaring. He kept it up until a hunter came along and shot him. The moral: WHEN YOU'RE FULL OF BULL, KEEP YOUR MOUTH SHUT.

IF YOU FIND
YOURSELF IN
A HOLE, THE
FIRST THING
TO DO IS STOP
DIGGIN'.

The easiest way to eat crow
is while it's still warm.

The colder it gets, the
harder it is to swaller.

NEVER SMACK A MAN WHO'S CHEWIN' TOBACCO.

If it don't
seem like
it's worth
the effort,
it probably
ain't.

NEVER GRUMBLE. It makes you about as welcome as a sidewinder in a cow camp.

It don't take a genius to spot a goat in a flock of sheep.

**WHEN DEALIN' WITH A
SLICK SON OF A BITCH,**

start off by pinnin' him down
and changin' his oil.

THE BIGGEST LIAR you'll ever
have to deal with probably watches
you shave his face in the mirror
every morning.

The best
way to
find a lost
stray is to
go to the
place you
would go if
you were a
lost stray.

NEVER ASK A BARBER IF HE THINKS YOU NEED A HAIRCUT.

If your guts have turned to fiddle
strings on the cowboy trail,

it ain't good for you and
it ain't safe for me.

NEVER FOLLOW
GOOD WHISKEY
WITH WATER,
UNLESS YOU'RE
OUT OF GOOD
WHISKEY.

If you get to thinkin' you're a person of some influence, try orderin' somebody else's dog around.

NEVER try to run a bluff when your poke's empty.

TALK LOW, TALK SLOW, AND DON'T SAY TOO MUCH.

A man with an edgy smile is
like a dog with a waggin' tail:
HE'S NOT HAPPY, HE'S NERVOUS.

DON'T WORRY
ABOUT BITING
OFF MORE
THAN YOU
CAN CHEW.
YOUR MOUTH
IS PROBABLY
A WHOLE LOT
BIGGER 'N
YOU THINK.

Good judgment
comes from
experience, and
a lot of that
comes from
bad judgment.

ALWAYS DRINK UPSTREAM FROM THE HERD.

Generally, you ain't learnin' nothin' when your mouth is a-jawin'.

Tellin' a man
to go to hell
and makin'
him do it are
two entirely
different
propositions.

MAKIN' IT IN LIFE
is kinda like bustin' broncs:
you're gonna get thrown a lot.
**THE SIMPLE SECRET IS TO
KEEP GETTIN' BACK ON.**

NEVER MISS A CHANCE TO REST YOUR HORSE.

THE BEST WAY TO COOK any
part of a rangy ol' longhorn is to
toss it in a pot with a horseshoe,
and when the horseshoe is soft and
tender, you can eat the beef.

Remain independent of any
source of income that will
DEPRIVE YOU OF YOUR
PERSONAL LIBERTIES.

★ ★ ★

GENERALLY
SPEAKING,
fancy
titles and
nightshirts
are a waste
of time.

NEVER DROP
YOUR GUN
TO HUG A GRIZZLY.

TRUST

EVERYBODY

in the game,

BUT

ALWAYS

cut the cards.

A woman's heart is like a campfire. If you don't tend to it regular, you'll soon lose it.

IF YOU'RE
RIDIN' AHEAD
OF THE HERD,
TAKE A LOOK
BACK EVERY
NOW AND
THEN TO MAKE
SURE IT'S
STILL THERE.

NO MATTER WHERE YOU RIDE TO, THAT'S WHERE YOU ARE.

WHEN YOU GIVE A LESSON
IN MEANNESS TO A
CRITTER OR A PERSON,
DON'T BE SURPRISED IF THEY
LEARN THEIR LESSON.

If you're gonna go,
GO LIKE HELL.

If your mind's not made up,
DON'T USE YOUR SPURS.

IF YOU'RE
SITTIN' AT
A COUNTER
EATIN', LEAVE
YOUR HAT ON.
IF YOU'RE
SITTIN' AT A
TABLE, TAKE
IT OFF.

A body can pretend to care, but they can't pretend to be there.

THE BEST WAY to have quiche
for dinner is to make it up and put
it in the oven to bake at about 325
degrees. Meanwhile, get out a large
T-bone, grill it, and when it's done,
eat it. As for the quiche, continue to
let it bake, but otherwise ignore it.

A lot of
good luck is
undeserved,

but then so
is a lot of
bad luck.

SOME THINGS AIN'T FUNNY.

You can just
about always
stand more'n
you think
you can.

IT DON'T
MATTER SO
MUCH HOW
LONG A RIDE
YOU HAVE,
AS HOW WELL
YOU RIDE IT.

WHEN IT COMES TO CUSSIN'

don't swallow your tongue;

Use both barrels

And air out your lungs.

A man who wants to loan you a slicker when it ain't rainin' ain't doin' much for you.

REMEMBER,
EVEN A KICK IN
THE CABOOSE
IS A STEP
FORWARD.

THERE'S ONLY TWO THINGS YOU NEED TO BE AFRAID OF:

A DECENT WOMAN AND BEIN' LEFT AFOOT.

There's two theories to arguin' with a woman.

NEITHER ONE WORKS.

If you expect
to follow the
trail, you must
do your sleepin'
in the winter.

IF YOU'RE GONNA drive cattle

through town, do it on a Sunday.

There's little traffic and people are

more prayerful and less disposed to

cuss at you.

Don't get
mad at
somebody
who knows
more'n
you do.
IT AIN'T
THEIR
FAULT.

THERE'S NO TIME TO REST when there's work to be done. Eat on the run, forget about sleep, and change horses often.

IF YOU'RE GONNA TAKE THE MEASURE OF A MAN, TAKE THE FULL MEASURE.

Egg shells
in the
coffee keep
it shy of
bitterness.

DON'T TAKE
OFF TOO MANY
CLOTHES WHEN
YOU BED DOWN
ON THE TRAIL.
YOU MIGHT
NEED TO DRESS
IN A HURRY.

ALWAYS
REMEMBER
YOUR HORSE
HEARS AND
SMELLS A
WHOLE LOT
MORE 'N
YOU DO.

NEVER GO to your room in the daytime.

When you're tryin' somethin' new, the fewer people who know about it, the better.

Just because
a man takes
his boots off
to go wadin'
don't mean he
plans to swim
the Atlantic.

★★★

Kickin' never gets you nowheres,
LESS'N YOU'RE A MULE.

THERE'S
NO PLACE
'ROUND THE
CAMPFIRE FOR
A QUITTER'S
BLANKET.

ONLY A BUZZARD FEEDS ON HIS FRIENDS.

Control
your
generosity
when you're
dealin' with
a chronic
borrower.

Don't squat with yer spurs on!

When you
throw your
weight around,
be ready to
have it thrown
around by
somebody else.

TOO MUCH
DEBT DOUBLES
THE WEIGHT
ON YOUR
HORSE AND
PUTS ANOTHER
IN CONTROL OF
THE REINS.

THERE'S NO SUCH THING as a sure thing. Let the other fellows run on the rope if they want to, but you keep your money in your pocket.

SPEAK YOUR MIND, BUT RIDE A FAST HORSE.

The length of
a conversation
don't tell
nothin' about
the size of
the intellect.

WHEN YOU'RE PUTTIN'
TOGETHER AN OUTFIT, take
your time. Wait for all the loose-lipped,
manicured cowboys to run their line
and wander off. Then make your picks
from the wiser heads who stayed around
listenin' and thinkin'.

NO MATTER
WHERE YOU
GO OR WHAT
YOU DO, KEEP
YOUR SADDLE
AND CHAPS
AND ALWAYS
KNOW WHERE
YOU CAN GET
A GOOD RIDE.

GO AFTER
LIFE AS IF IT'S
SOMETHING
THAT'S GOT TO
BE ROPED IN A
HURRY BEFORE
IT GETS AWAY.

WORKIN' BEHIND A PLOW, all
you see is a mule's hind end. Workin'
from the back of a horse, you can
see across the country as far as
your eye is good.

Solvin' problems is like throwin' cattle. Dig your heels in on the big ones and catch the little ones 'round the neck.

NEVER RIDE WITH A SADDLE STIFF. HE WILL PREY ON YOUR HONESTY AND LOYALTY.

THE BASICS OF ROPING are a sense of rhythm, good timing, and an eye for distance. You might also wanta keep this in mind when you're two-steppin' around the dance floor.

The only
way to drive
cattle fast
is slowly.

NEVER RUN FROM A FIGHT.

If you're gonna get hit, it's better
to take it in the front than in
the back—and it looks better.

LETTIN' THE
CAT OUT OF
THE BAG IS
A WHOLE
LOT EASIER
'N PUTTIN'
IT BACK.

Don't let so much reality into your life that there's no room left for dreamin'.

ALWAYS TAKE A GOOD LOOK at what you're about to eat. It's not so important to know what it is, but it's critical to know what it was.

A person
who agrees
with
all your
palaver
is either a
fool or he's
gettin' ready
to skin ya.

ALWAYS CARRY MORE 'N ONE ROPE.

You might run across more
'n one rope can handle.

AIN'T NEVER SEEN A WILD CRITTER FEELIN' SORRY FOR ITSELF.

The quickest
way to double
your money is
to fold it over
and put it back
in your pocket.

MOST FOLKS are like a bob-wire fence. They have their good points.

IF YOU WANT TO HAVE A DRINK OR TWO,

that's all right—but don't wear out
your boot soles on a brass rail.

NEVER MISS A GOOD CHANCE TO SHUT UP.

THE BEST WAY TO KEEP YOUR WORD IS NOT TO GIVE IT FOOLISHLY.

IF YOU DRINK TEQUILA,
don't dive off the sidewalk. Most
generally the water is too low, and
in nine out of ten towns, there is at
least a $50 fine for it.

There's a lot
more to ridin'
a horse than
just sittin' in
the saddle and
lettin' yer feet
hang down.

NOBODY EVER DROWNED HIMSELF IN HIS OWN SWEAT.

No tree is
too big for
a short dog
to lift his
leg on.

YOU DON'T NEED DECORATED WORDS TO MAKE YOUR MEANIN' CLEAR. SAY IT PLAIN AND SAVE SOME BREATH FOR BREATHIN'.

TWO DRY LOGS WILL BURN A GREEN ONE.

NEVER LIE
unless you
have to,
and if you
don't have a
damn good
lie, stick to
the truth.

IF YOU WORK FOR A MAN, RIDE FOR HIS BRAND.

Treat his cattle as if
they were your own.

TO GET A HANDLE on modern French philosophers, just assume that everything nonphysical is real, while everything of substance is unreal. So, sadness is real, but escargot is not.

When you get
to where you're
goin', the first
thing to do is
take care of
the horse you
rode in on.

HONESTY IS NOT SOMETHIN' YOU SHOULD FLIRT WITH. YOU SHOULD BE MARRIED TO IT.

WET DOGS ARE NEVER WELCOME.

It doesn't
matter how
fast you are if
the other guy
is so much as
a hair faster.

DEPENDING ON THE CIRCUMSTANCES, you can tolerate a certain amount of slick-eared calf poachin', but horse stealin' is a hangin' offense.

WEAR A HAT WITH A BRIM
WIDE ENOUGH TO SHED SUN
AND RAIN, FAN A CAMPFIRE,
DIP WATER, AND WHIP A
FIGHTIN' COW IN THE FACE.

You can't
always tell
a gunslinger
by the way
he walks.

ANY COWBOY
WORTH HIS
SALT HAS A
ROPE HAND
THAT ITCHES
CLEAN UP TO
HIS SHOULDER
BONE.

WHEN YOU'RE PICKIN' A WORKIN' HORSE, look for one named Screwtail, Stump Sucker, Rat's Ass, Pearly Gates, Liver Pill, or Darlin' Jill. Leave the Champions and Silvers for the show ring.

YOU CAN NEVER STEP IN THE SAME RIVER TWICE.

Never take
another
man's bet. He
wouldn't offer
it if he didn't
know somethin'
you don't.

Any time
a large
herd moves
through a
civilized
area there's
A LOT OF
SHIT to
clean up.

COOLNESS AND A STEADY NERVE
will always beat simple quickness.
Take yer time and you'll only need
to PULL THE TRIGGER ONCE.

A center-fire rig won't do on
steep trails. So when you're
in rimfire country, always
double-cinch your saddle.

NEVER GET
UP BEFORE
BREAKFAST.
IF YOU HAVE TO
GET UP BEFORE
BREAKFAST,
EAT
BREAKFAST
FIRST.

If you want to forget all your troubles, take a little walk in a brand-new pair of high-heeled ridin' boots.

COMIN' AS CLOSE TO THE TRUTH
as a man can come without actually
gettin' there is comin' pretty close,
but it still ain't the truth.

NEVER JOKE WITH
MULES OR COOKS

AS THEY HAVE NO
SENSE OF HUMOR.

THE FIRST
THING TO DO
when you
get up in the
morning is
put on your
Stetson.

ALWAYS TRY
TO BE A BIT
NICER THAN IS
CALLED FOR,
BUT DON'T
TAKE TOO
MUCH GUFF.

IT'S BEST to keep your troubles pretty much to yourself, 'cause half the people you'd tell 'em to won't give a damn, and the other half will be glad to hear you've got 'em.

Don't ask friends for more'n they would give on their own.

It's better to sit on your horse and do nothing than to wear him out chasin' shadows.

PICK THE RIGHT HORSE FOR THE JOB.

THE COWBOY, WHO EXAGGERATES TOO MUCH soon finds that everyone else has left the campfire.

IT'S RARE
TO FIND A
HORSE THAT
EVERYONE
AGREES IS
THE BEST IN
THE HERD.

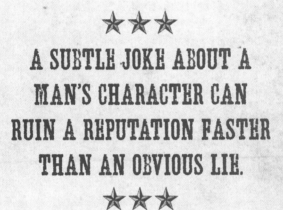

★★★

A SUBTLE JOKE ABOUT A
MAN'S CHARACTER CAN
RUIN A REPUTATION FASTER
THAN AN OBVIOUS LIE.

★★★

Nothin's better than a cool drink of water—but too much can give you a bellyache.

ON THE RANGE, an unlocked ranch house is an invitation to a weary cowboy to help himself to food and shelter. Cash payment for this kind of hospitality is a serious breach of etiquette. A note of thanks and payment in kind is all that is expected.

NO MATTER WHO SAYS WHAT, DON'T BELIEVE IT IF IT DON'T MAKE SENSE.

A SMART
ASS
just don't fit
in a saddle.

THE WILDEST CRITTERS LIVE IN THE CITY!